Porgy's Revenge

Porgy's Revenge
Erika Abbott

Illustrated by
Kyle, Amelia, and Logan Behan

ARCHWAY PUBLISHING

Copyright © 2015 Erika Abbott.

All rights reserved. No part of this book may be used or reproduced by any means, graphic, electronic, or mechanical, including photocopying, recording, taping or by any information storage retrieval system without the written permission of the author except in the case of brief quotations embodied in critical articles and reviews.

Archway Publishing books may be ordered through booksellers or by contacting:

Archway Publishing
1663 Liberty Drive
Bloomington, IN 47403
www.archwaypublishing.com
1 (888) 242-5904

Because of the dynamic nature of the Internet, any web addresses or links contained in this book may have changed since publication and may no longer be valid. The views expressed in this work are solely those of the author and do not necessarily reflect the views of the publisher, and the publisher hereby disclaims any responsibility for them.

Any people depicted in stock imagery provided by Thinkstock are models, and such images are being used for illustrative purposes only.
Certain stock imagery © Thinkstock.

ISBN: 978-1-4808-2333-4 (sc)
ISBN: 978-1-4808-2375-4 (hc)
ISBN: 978-1-4808-2334-1 (e)

Library of Congress Control Number: 2015916703

Print information available on the last page.

Archway Publishing rev. date: 10/26/2015

Dedications

First of all, I want to dedicate this book to my two nephews, Kyle and Logan, and my beautiful niece, Amelia. Thanks for doing the artwork, kids! A huge dedication to Zoe Abbott Behan, my sister, and my brother-in-law Ruark, who are raising my two nephews and my one niece, with grace, patience, and lots of humor.

Second, I'd like to dedicate this book to Joel Zwick, godfather, mentor, friend. Without his dedication to my poetry, and to me, this chapbook, would indeed, have stayed just a dream.

To John Rubinstein, who starred in "Pippin" in 1971. Because of him, two of my poems were inspired by "Pippin." One called "Pippin", the other called "War." Thanks, John.

I'd also like to dedicate this book to Charley Roth. Charley was my first friend. I knew him before I ever met Aaron. Charley was born on September 16, 1971, and his promise died with him on April 18, 1983. He was 11.5 years old. I love you, Charley.

A huge dedication to my parents: Ron and Annie Abbott, who gave me all the support I ever needed, an amazing education in the arts(which took me farther than I ever could have imagined), and a wonderful love of Jazz! Thanks, mom and dad!

Finally, to my "Porgy and Bess" family.....Aaron Seglin, Monica Gaines, all the kids in Phil Stern's House Y Social Studies Class, thanks. You inspire me every day.

Contents

Allegory • 1
Panorama • 5
A Famous Poet Once Wrote • 6
Porgy and Bess • 8
I Am Your • 14
Jagger • 19
Master • 20
The Invisible Fool • 21
Hamlet • 23
Personal Ad • 25
Shames • 27
Sesame Oil • 32
Steam • 34
Fully Dressed • 38
Catch Me • 44

Criminal Kabbalah • 48
Cliffhanger • 49
The Last Kiss • 52
Chessboard • 54
A-bomb* • 61
Shakespeare • 63
The Promise • 69
July 8, 2001** • 72
Mutilation.doc • 74
Ophelia's Technicolor G-String: An Urban Tradition • 77
Mystery Dance • 81
Always • 82
Lubbock, Texas • 88
Pippin • 89
The Secrets of Children • 94
These Days • 96
War • 97

  * Poem by Ronald Abbott
 ** Poem by Ann Rita Abbott

Introduction

Over the past year, as I compiled this poetry collection, many of my friends asked me "Why now, Erika? Why this selection of poems?"

The Ugly Laws are my answer: "Any person who is diseased, maimed, mutilated, or in any way, deformed so as to be an unsightly or improper person to be allowed in or on our streets, shall be fined $1 for each offense."

Growing up in Montclair, NJ, in the mid-1970's, and early 1980's, my friends and I didn't realize we were still being Annexed!

Allegory

The
Evening
He
Bundled
Me
Up,
The
Purple
Veins
Immobilized
On
The
Nape
Of
His
Neck
Like
Ropes.
At
That
Moment,
I
Grieved
For

My
"Happily
Ever
After."
I
Was
Three
When
I
Started
To
Jitterbug
With
Poets
And
Bookish
Folk.
But,
In
My
Thirties,
I
Speculated,
Where
Are
Today's
Knights?

And
Marveled
At
The
Punishing
And
Striking
Of
A
Poor
Rag
Doll
Makes
The
Headlines ...
As
It
Becomes
Painfully
Clear
That
Sometimes
Life
Is
A
Poor
Allegory.

Picture of Knight by Kyle Behan, Age 9

Panorama

Kaleidoscopes of arsenic wishes
Part the way to Yankee Stadium
As though reweaving the American Dream.
I watch quick bursts of color loom through the sky.
Johnny One-Note came marching home
To a symphony along the waterfront,
money changing hands,
Inundated by the domination of easy money.
The aroma of the low-down blues wafts,
floats over the rose growing in cement.
As Mother Nature briefly paints a canvas, going
from midnight red to smoky sapphire-raven,
I walk down Forty-Second Street,
A school of hookers luring their bait
While they crave that kind of love.
Initiation is Kafkaesque;
Circle of life continues—
No white gardenias here.
Diaries are written in blood;
Keepsakes are emblazoned on the body.
Players in this nightclub
Have extended contracts.
No Romeo here—
Just cheese, snow,
"True love."

A Famous Poet Once Wrote

A famous poet once wrote,
"Nothing gold can stay."
I watch a crowd of six-year-olds,
The progeny of East LA.
One by one, they ask me
Why my hand was curled.
I said, "That's the way
I was born into this world."
They looked at me and smiled
And went on their merry way—
Except for one. His face deadpanned.
He blinked at me to see the shape
Of
The piece of paper that from my holding fell.
He studied its unfolding
And said, "That's a trip.
Were you born with that
In your grip as well?"

Picture by Kyle Behan, age 9

Porgy and Bess

It was the dress rehearsal, the *Porgy and Bess* rehearsal;
tomorrow was the show—
But stuff had been tough that year on
Cafdish Row.
Creeping in my window
Since my man done gone.
She was a loud-spoken girl
With a lot of, well, you know.
But not today.
Hey, did you hear what went down?
No, what?
Check it out; you gonna bug.
Rumors didn't spread half as fast in Hollywood as they did in
the Lunchroom … as they did in Cafdish Row.
He told her he'd take her to town.
No way, who?
Sistrunk.
She wadn't wi' him, no way.
Yeah, she was. It was just a charity case.
Chorus for the church scene, on in two!
I'm talking to you!
Hey, did you hear?
No, what?
Sistrunk.
What'd he do now?
He was selling dimes to kids at Watchung.

Naw man, really?
Yeah, heard it my own damn self
From—you know, that kid.
You know the one. *Sssh!*
Did you hear?
No, what?
She scamming someone
Else every week.
Naw man, really?
Don't you never let
No woman claim you
Just because she got
Your wedding ring.
A woman is a
Sometimes thing.
There we were,
Sitting in Social Science,
rappin' 'bout the ins and outs,
'Specially after the defiance,
Shouts of Joan
And all the women who stood alone.
Summertime,
And the livin' is easy.
Fish are jumping, and the
Cotton is high.
Bess standing there
With a single spotlight bare,
As the small girl stands and sings

In dulcet tone.
As the final bell rings appeal,
Our heroine goes home to things
Much more real—
Like the drama of Bess' Catfish Row:
No peace, no mama.
Yeah, you know the deal.
Sportin' life goes his crooked way.
No fear, he's in the clear another day.
The stagehands and the crew
Have plans to do what such
Folks do.
Porgy goes with Bess,
But he will not hear her express
concern when stopping at her place.
Life teaches her to hide her fear
From those like him
She holds most dear.
Crown, on stage!
This is your big scene.
This is where you go
From someone who is to
someone who's been.
The ring of the bell—
Everything starting all
Over again.
Kids talking,
Teachers yell.

Hey, did you hear?
Porgy went home
with Bess yesterday.
For real, man?
Yeah, heard it
My own damn self from my older sister …
You know the one. *Ssssh!*
Back in social science, we were trying to unravel
Quite the mystery
'Bout why blacks had to raise the cry
And stop the gavel
From hammering on their history
And on their freedoms when they'd
Travel on a train or bus.
But some in the class were sayin'
Justice has not come to pass,
You see, and had to explain,
"That's her, that's me, that's us."
What's up wi' that? You have white skin.
Yes, but my limp makes me one of
Porgy's kin.
Meanwhile, back in Cafdish Row,
What'd you guys think
Of that weird girl in Soc today?
Was that a trip or what? Well, yeah,
She kinda flipped, but she made some points. Hey, when did you Become weird? People are people. Shut up, G! I swear I'm 'bout

To explode if I hear that song by Depeche Commode.
So, is there any of this junk you
Want to eat today?
No, I don't think so. No, they'll have some humble pie or a piece of Crow.
You and us on the set …
Oh, I'm sorry—don't you have to fix
That hair yet?
Meanwhile, back under the lights,
they put aside for now their fights.
There were only some five days left.
That jacket's deft!
Where's Sportin' Life?
All right, go to makeup
You're on in two.
Bess, where are you?
There's a boat that's leavin' soon
For New York.
Sister, come with me.
The next night, the curtain rose
Promptly at eight.
It was the end of a year of hurry up
And wait.
From summertime to start of spring
And havin' plenty of nothing,
With school year ending soon—
And then how would Bess ever
Become my woman now?

Picture of Monica Gaines, Inspiration for Poem

I Am Your

I
Am
Your
Crippled
Poet,
But
I
Am
Not
Browning.
I
Am
Your
Soothsayer
And
Painter,
Full
Of
Extravagant
Passages,
Perceptions,
While

Depicting
The
Panorama
Of
My
Soul
And
The
Spirit
Of
Humanity.
I
Am
Developing
A
Patchwork,
Chanting
Of
The
Downtrodden
Proletariat.
I
Am
A

Fool
Telling
The
Monarch
What
He
Doesn't
Require
To
Probe.
I
Dine
Excellently,
Fantasize
Creatively.
I
Once
Knew
Superstition.
I
Experience
The
Universe,
Employ

It
As
Grist
For
My
Mill.
Humanity
Is
A
Mirage,
And
I'm
Dreaming
It
All—
The
Benevolence,
The
Barbarity.
I
Weave
A
Beauteous,
Painful

Illustration
Of
The
Coarse
Populace.
If
I
Remove
My
Facade,
Before
Long,
I'll
See
The
Real
World
That
Has
Permeated
My
Reverence.

Jagger

"It
Was
The
Best
Thing
I
Ever
Got
Out
Of
A
Relationship,"
She
Told
Me.
Well,
The
Second
Best,
Anyway ...
Jagger's
Lips
Kept
Her
Secrets.

Master

Spinoza
Dreams
Text,
Cleric
Of
Philosophy.
Puzzlement
Reigns
As
Your
Temples
Are
Transformed
To
Garages.
Consequently,
You
Have
Been
Distorted
Into
RAM.

The Invisible Fool

The
Folds
From
Her
Stomach
Overhang
As
She
Pulls
Her
Jeans
Over
Her
Annoyance.
I
Watch
As
She
Performs
The
Ballet
Of

Pulling
Down
The
Shirt,
Pulling
Up
The
Jeans.
In
This
World,
She
Is
The
Invisible
Fool.

Hamlet

A
Howl
Of
Brakes—
Or
Is
It
A
Birth
Shriek?
The
Daring
Of
The
Secure
Mouths,

Laden
As
They
Are
With
Bastardies.
Sweet
Hamlet,
Where
Do
You
Stockpile
Your
Life?

Personal Ad

Poet
Craves
A
Lover,
Partner,
Confidant,
Passionate
Soul
With
Vast
Intellect,
Courage
To
Share
Bed,
To
Help
Motivate
Humankind,
To
Triumph

Over
World
Anger
And
Guilt,
Empowered
By
Whitman,
Blake,
Gershwin,
And
Sondheim.
Poet,
Yuppie,
Or
Scholar,
Find
Me
In
Los
Angeles
Alone.

Shames

A
Child
Stands
Up,
And
He's
Big
Enough
Now
To
Understand
How
He
Can
Hurl
Some
Names,
Inflict
Some
Shames,
Calling
People
Spic,
Nigger,
Or

Jew,
Bastard.
Apparently,
This
Child's
Mastered
The
Seed
Of
Ways
That
Give
Birth
To
Burning
Days
Above
South
Africas
Or
South
Central
LAs.
So,
How
To

Prevent
These
Displays?
I
Teach
Them.
I
Try
To
Reach
Them
Before
The
Bullies
In
The
Schoolyard
Bleach
Their
Minds
Or
Beat
Their
Behinds.
I
Beseech

Them,
Try
To
Look
For
Signs
Of
Hope,
To
Appreciate
That
This
Doesn't
Have
To
Be
Their
Fate.
The
Terror,
The
Technines,
And
The
Dope.
I

Tell
Them,
On
The
Thought,
There
Is
A
Reason
Great
Names
Fought
For
Each
And
Every
Great
Idea
When
They
Ask
Themselves
And
Us,
"Why
Here?"

Sesame Oil

The
Sesame
Oil
You
Brought
Me
To
Knead
Me
Into
Your
Skin
Composes
Firelight.
You
Kissed
My
Frame
To
A
Cloud—
Stratus,
Cirrus,
Nimbus.
Now,
Moving

Balls
From
Your
Pulse
Points,
Calling
Up
The
Blood
To
Your
Facade,
I
Utilize
My
Hands
To
Lavish
Your
Physique,
Secreted
Here
By
A
Vermillion
Perimeter
Of
Quilt.

Steam

Heat—
Let's
Heat
Up
The
Dusk
To
A
Boil.
Let's
Steam
Every
Ounce
Of
Our
Flesh
Till
We
Crackle,
Not
A
Globule
Of
Approach

Present.
We
Are
Saucepans
On
Too
High,
A
Blaze;
Our
Insides
Char,
Flake—
Murky,
Like
Sinister
Snowstorms.
Idling
Down,
We
Exhale
Smoke.
We
Expire;

Slumber
Envelops
Us
In
Ruins.
We
Recline
Without
Fantasizing,
Vacant
As
Stepford
Wives.
Yet
We
Awaken,
Clattering
As
Waterfalls
Soar
Off,
Hastening
Into
The

Nocturnal,
Thundering
Into
Our
Dazzling
Intentions.
It
Is
The
Old
Yiddish
Song:
What
Can
Combust
And
Not
Burn
Up?
Passion
That
Renews
Itself
Daily.

Fully Dressed

You're
Never
Fully
Dressed
Without
A
Smile.
Looking
For
Horton
While
Livin'
With
The
King.
He
Beat
Me
Black,
Blue,
Purple;
I
Riffed

It
Out
O'
There
With
My
Handyman,
Walkin'
Down
The
Yellow
Brick
Road
To
High
Society.
I
Found
The
Great
Glass
Elevator.
Ella,
Henny
Went

All
Over
Town
With
Charley
And
Me.
Yesterday,
On
Our
Travels,
We
Found
Something
Mysterious—
The
Nettibeast,
Paralyzed
With
Fear,
A
Sense
Of
Wonder.
"Do

Not
Be
Afraid,
My
Child;
I
Am
Just
Your
Guide."
Buying
Tickets
On
The
Atchison,
Topeka,
And
The
Santa
Fe
For
Guests
Coming
To
Dinner

In
The
Heat
Of
The
Night.
Anything
Goes
On
34th
Street—
Cacophonous
Orgies
Of
Pennies
Falling
From
The
Heavens
As
We
Marveled
Over
The
Moors,

Magic
Dripping
From
Every
Bulb.
We
Climbed
Aboard
The
A
Train
In
A
Mist
Of
Avalon,
Watching
A
Fox
In
Socks
Give
An
Inaugural
Address.

Catch Me

Catch me,
Catch me
If
You
Dare,
On
An
Odyssey
To
Meet
Mother
Courage.
Catch
Me
Dancing
The
Hora
In
The
Ghetto,

If
You
Dare,
On
Stage
In
The
Theater
Of
The
Oppressed.
Catch
Me,
Catch
Me
Tempting
Men
With
A
Sex
Strike.

Catch
Me
Helping
Nora
Slam
The
Door.
If
You
Dare,
Catch
Me.
Catch
Me
Stealing
The
Moon
While
Plato
Corrupted
The
Minds

Of
Greek
Youths,
If
You
Dare.
Catch
Me
Crossing
Delancey
In
The
Good
Old
Summertime.
Catch
Me,
Catch
Me,
If
You
Dare …

Criminal Kabbalah

Rashi's
Daughters
Were
Taught
Criminal
Kabbalah.
So
Began
Their
Plunge
Into
Torture,
Otherwise
Branded
As
Finding
Husbands.

Cliffhanger

Once
Upon
A
Time
In
A
Land
Long
Forgotten
Among
The
Nebulous
Azure
Ebony
Mountains
Crimson
Rain
Started
The
Apocalypse.
The
Enduring

History
Obscures
Her
Mind,
A
Labyrinth
From
Which
She
Cannot
Escape.
The
Ancient
Foreign
Voices
Echo
To
Her.
She
Can
No
Longer
Hear

Their
Mystery. ...
Exhaustion
Now
Navigates
Her
Voyage.
As
Her
Descendants
Maintain
The
Legacy,
The
Welcome
Wagon
Of
Cherished
Loved
Ones
Returns
Her
Home.

The Last Kiss

The
Story
Beguiles
Our
Days
With
Wine.
Roses
We
Slip
Gently
Past
To
Overtures
Of
Love—
People
Laughing,
Talking,
Sharing
Stories.

He
Rises,
Leaning
Over
The
Forest
Green
Couch,
Gives
Her
The
Last
Kiss
They
Will
Ever
Share.

Chessboard

Maybe
We'll
Procure
The
Chessboard
For
When
He
Comes
Home
To
Play
Once
More.
The
Tray
Stand
Careened
Over
His
Sheeted
Lap
Like
Mine
When
I

Was
Eight
And
Sick,
Too
Sick,
To
Enjoy
Lying
On
The
Sofa
In
The
Living
Room
And
Contemplating
TV.
I
Recollect
The
Focus
In
His
Face,
Stooped

Over,
The
Black
And
White
Sheet
Of
Rules.
For
Hours
Across
The
Room
Seahorses
Moved
In
A
Saltwater
Tank,
Lithe
In
Water
As
If
A
Span

Of
Knights
Had
Vaulted
Them
Off
Their
Plastic
Stands.
In
The
Beginning,
He
Always
Won.
I
Couldn't
Tell
Where
We
Left
Off,
And
The
Game
Commenced.

Wandering
In
And
Out
Of
My
Skin,
I
Heard
Her
Reverberate
The
Kitchen
Pots.
Or
I
Thought
I
Heard
Her
Gliding
Like
A
Queen,
Across
The

Checkered
Floor,
Up
The
Mystic
Diagonals
Of
Tile,
And
Out
The
Door,
Where
Dad
Was
Arriving
Home,
One
Dignified
Sidewalk
Square
At
A
Time:
Our
King.

Picture of Rook by Kyle Behan

A-bomb

With morning's first light comes security.

The forms that I strained to perceive with my eyes and ears
in the receding
                       darkness

              reveal themselves.

        Annie, next, thick and solid.

      There is for me a special eagle-pride about
          waking while my brood sleeps.

     Annie, I love to see your face at rest, to be
        free to explore the curved plane

   Where nose meets cheek, cheek meets jaw, and so on.

And the same kind of thrill runs through
me as the children sleep.

My dragons wake me, and as they invade my mind and
stomach, I try to ignore them, wrestle with them, and once
or twice (but no more) even succeed in chasing them.

It is not hard to think how the same kind of
mind that thought to make a house
could also think to make the A-bomb, but it is hard to think
why he would want to.

Ron Abbott, Montclair, New Jersey

Shakespeare

The
Entire
Heavens
Are
A
Cliff
We
All
Imbibe
From
History's
Goblet
As
We
Libate
From
Camelot's
Global
Goblet.
The
Cobbled
Stones
Bloomed
Like
Children.

I trod on,
Had roughly surfaced the remains
I dug encompassing him.
I sheltered him myself.
Today every day is a cemetery that must be protected.
And
You
Must
Beware
Of
The
Orphaned
Avenue
Full
Of
Drugs,
Mattress
Coverings,
Garbage.
For
My brother,
Even
Now
I
Add
Every
Point

In
The
Wire.
The
Stars
Were
Protected
With
The
Sandstorm
Of
The
Briars
Of
Rage.
You
Want
To
Cleanse
Revenge
From
Your
Eyes.
Shakespeare
Kept
Observing
Me,

As
A
Hunchback,
Caterwauling
Excitedly.
In
Another
Dwelling,
A
Crowd
Of
Birds
Breaks
Itself
Apart
To
Alert
The
King
Of
What
Will
Befall
His
State.
What
I

Categorized
Was
A
New
Expression
For
Fairness,
A
New
Lexicon
For
Love.
What
I
Ventured
To
Disguise
With
Ashes
Was
Hate,
Revenge.
Yet
You
Can
See
Revenge

In
All
Mass
Graves
Everywhere.
It
Turns
Out
I
Buried
Myself.
We
Are
All
Buried
Alive
In
The
Chamber
Of
Someone
Else's
Heart.

The Promise

In
A
Galaxy
Long
Ago
And
Far
Away,
Where
Dreams
Were
Voiced,
Tomorrow
Came,
But
He
Never
Did
"NO!"

Still
Innocent,
The
Promise
Was
Made.
"I'll
See
You
Tomorrow,"
He
Said.
Tomorrow
Approached,
But
He
Never
Did.

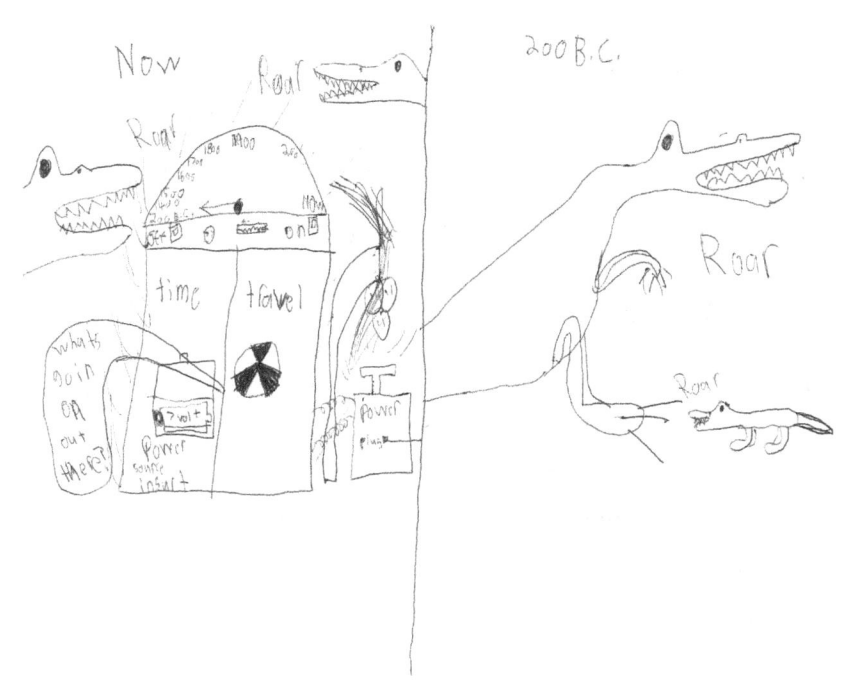

Picture of Dinosaurs Time Traveling by Kyle Behan

July 8, 2001

Our silver fish, scales gleaming in flight,

Soars

Diving thru clouds, whose moisture, heavy in repose,

Bursts free

Spraying the odd planet, the sudden
meteor in its determined flight,

Exploding thru the universe and on and on,

Racing the shore to the horizon.

Our silver fish

Splashes stars in its ascent,

Shooting past all known formations,
shaking loose the seaweed, the fauna,

From the earth's floor.

Nestled in a bubble, there—

To dangle, to spin, to tiptoe atop a molecule of air,

Free of weight, of form, of judgment.

Our silver fish rides to ragged surf to calm,

Shaking free the sands of ridicule,

Hurdling high—past expectation, on—

To wonder

There to rest

Find peace

Suckle at the breast of creation.
Embraced, the artist endures.

July 8, 2001 written by Annie Abbott,
is about the poet's birth

Mutilation.doc

Nearby
Is
A
Limb
In
The
Thoroughfare.
It
Is
Diminutive;
Should
Be
Attached
To
A
Five
Year
Old.
You
Cannot
Distinguish
If
The
Hand
Belongs
To

A
Palestinian
Or
Israeli
Kid.
You
Cannot
Discriminate
If
These
Limbs
Drifted
Here
From
A
Suicide
Bombing.
A
Miniature
Blood
Spattered
Hand ...
We are
Counseled
It's
Simply
Collateral
Mutilation

Picture of Hearts by Amelia Behan, Age 6

Ophelia's Technicolor G-String: An Urban Tradition

Hamlet,
If
You
Could
Witness
Me
As
I
Swagger
Across
The
Amphitheater,
Shawl
Dripping
Through
The
Floorboards,
Me
In
Stilettos
And
A
Technicolor
G-string,

You
Would
Not
Wish
Thee
To
A
Nunnery.
Here,
I
Am
Queen,
My
Spouse
A
Pint
Of
Gin.
Someday
I
Divine
Finding
You
Here,
Flanked

At
The
Tables
On
Conti,
Bourbon
Streets,
Radiating
Me
A
Marlboro.
Now
I
Dance
For
Claudius,
Since
Only
He
Recognizes
Me
As
Horatio
In
Drag.

Picture of Snowman with Snow Falling and
Hearts and Trees, by Logan Behan

Mystery Dance

We
Force
Ourselves
Together
Like
Two
Edge
Pieces
Of
A
Puzzle,
Attempting
To
Find
Our
Way
Through
This
Mystery
Dance
We
Call
Life.

Always

First
To
Rise
In
The
Beginning
I
Travel
In
Honeysuckle
Time
To
Visit
Harry
Over
The
River
Jordan
In
The
Banana
Boats
In
The

Shtetl
And
Even
In
The
Ghetto
Syncopating
In
Blue,
Basking
In
Holy
Moonlight,
Always
First
To
Rise
In
The
Beginning
Like
A
Phoenix
With
Red
Hot

Feet,
Always
First
To
Rise
In
Blue
Jeans
And
Socks,
Clawing
To
Break
Free,
Tripping
Amid
A
Kaleidoscope
Of
Strange
Bodies.
He
Fed
Me
A
Steady

Diet
Of
Jazz.
This
Is
Ted
Brown,
The
Morning
Man
On
WNEW.
The
Most
Magical
Mystical
Mysterious
Part
Of
My
Education
Had
Just
Begun.
This
Is

Ted
Brown
The
Morning
Man
On
WNEW,
Purchasing
A
Ticket
For
You
To
Ride
The
Train
With
Mack
The
Knife
To
Catfish
Row.

Picture of the Universe by Logan Behan, Age 5

Lubbock, Texas*

the immigrants have landed again
in a time searching for answers to long-ago questions,
swapping stories bathed in the glow of the eternal light,
recipes for okra,
dybbuks await me at every turn,
clouds move in
as if being choreographed,
der emes iz der besten lign,
time freezes
in a location
where cotton sings its sorrowful songs,
but them that sings them
sings loud and long,
the gin weaves broken dreams of yesterday.

---

* This poem took place at a music festival, in Lubbock, Texas.

Pippin

We've
Got
Magic
To
Do,
Just
For
You.
As
The
Global
Stage
Continues,
Inhabit
A
World
Even
The
Players
Could

Not
Have
Scripted.
Lysistrata
Stands
Screaming
At
The
Door
For
Peace,
But
Nobody
Can
Hear
Her
Because
Of
The
Wiretaps.
The
Gods
Must

Be
Crazy
To
Trust
Us
With
Our
Own
Lives.
Murder,
Mayhem,
All
In
The
Name
Of
"Good
Clean
Fun."
"Did
You
See
The

Neck
Contorted
Like
A
Figure
Eight?"
Someone
Asks.
People
Care,
But
Not
Enough
To
Call
911
For
The
Soul
Who's
Been
There
For
An

Eon,
Or
Since
Yesterday.
During
The
Long
Walk
Home,
Society
Says,
"Stop
Tormenting
Hard
Working
People
Like
Us.
Quit
Devastating
Everybody's
Perpetual
Summer."

The Secrets of Children

Whispers through the hidden playground
As we sojourn, fantasize, create, time-travel

Tripping amid a kaleidoscope of ricocheting bodies
Watching a war no one reports …

While we swam among an ocean of trepidation,

We forgot ourselves. We didn't know.

The secrets of children resonate, "Stop, it's not safe."

Some are malevolent; others still abhor.
The secrets of children raced

As bullets ricocheted through the whitewashed sky.
But we paid no heed;
We were too busy

Raping the system,
killing spirits,

While the secrets of children
Were kept to themselves.

We were busy
paying lip service,
bills,

Working
putting food on the table.

What red-blooded parent
Has time to sit down and
Waste precious time listening to
The secrets of children?

These Days

These days

Whatever you say,

Keep your heart honest.

I am a mystic, born with a third eye into the soul.

These days

Be careful what you say; children will listen.

Be careful what you do; children will see and learn.

War

War
Is
Business.
Invest
Your
Sons.
Oh
The
Judgment
Of
Statues
Attached
To
The
Tongues
Of
Gentlemen
While
At
Home
In

Many
Languages
The
Sun
Illuminates
Us.
In
The
Wind
A
Linden
Tree
Whispers,
"Military
Commanders
In
The
Field
Must
Have
Discretion
While
Stationary

Through
The
Onslaught."
Rumors
Of
Peace
Sent
The
Market
Spiraling.
A
Violin
Plays,
Flanked
By
Bulletins,
As
All
Things
Are
Considered
And
Reconsidered.

About the Author

Erika Abbott is a native of Manhattan, raised in Montclair, New Jersey. She earned a B.A. in literature from the University of Judaism and was invited to join the California Writers Club. She has been recognized by Beyond Baroque as one of the up and coming poets in Southern California, and her work has appeared in The Big Picture, MindfireRenew.com, and The Poet's Pen.

CPSIA information can be obtained
at www.ICGtesting.com
Printed in the USA
BVHW030529140821
614143BV00001B/130